THE
METRONOME
METHOD

THE
METRONOME
METHOD

A Fun Approach to Succession and Estate Planning for Family Enterprises

Hugh MacDonald
CPA, CA, CLU, TEP, FEA

iUniverse LLC
Bloomington

THE METRONOME METHOD
A Fun Approach to Succession and Estate Planning for Family Enterprises

iUniverse books may be ordered through booksellers or by contacting:

iUniverse LLC
1663 Liberty Drive
Bloomington, IN 47403
www.iuniverse.com
1-800-Authors (1-800-288-4677)

ISBN: 978-1-4917-0081-5 (sc)
ISBN: 978-1-4917-0083-9 (hc)
ISBN: 978-1-4917-0082-2 (ebk)

Library of Congress Control Number: 2013914319

Printed in the United States of America

iUniverse rev. date: 08/16/2013

CONTENTS

TESTIMONIALS

"Hugh has taken a truly novel 'downhome' sensible approach—the 'Metronome Method'—to make the important issue of succession and estate planning for family enterprise fun and practical—not something to be dreaded and delayed . . ."

**Jim Eisenhauer, CEO, ABCO
Group Limited (2nd generation)**

"The Metronome Method brings the subject of estate planning within a family context down to a readable level, where every business owner and their family can visualize the steps that they need to take in order to maintain peace and harmony within their family and to ensure a smooth transition of the business down through the generations."

**Larry Smith, Owner
Kathbern Management**

"Any family business, regardless of size, would benefit from heeding the practical and sage advice contained in 'The Metronome Method'—it will help ensure the future of your business, but more importantly, your family"

**Paul B. MacDonald, Executive Director
Canadian Association of Family Enterprise**

INTRODUCTION

THE METRONOME METHOD

I remember a meeting I was invited to a number of years ago by a husband and wife team representing the two active owners of a substantial family enterprise. The purpose of the meeting was to help these owners put their affairs in order from a succession and estate planning point of view. Predictably, the owners and their advisors quickly focused the meeting on tax, legal, insurance and money issues. It was also disclosed to me that the family business was up for sale, but this fact was perceived to be so confidential that Mom and Dad had not yet told their son who was also their General Manager.

Let's pretend that this is a university communications class and your assignment as students is to identify any issues uncovered by this little case which might have unintended consequences to the family business and to the family relationships. Can you think of any issues? I can think of a few which I will share with you throughout the book.

Why did I write this book?

In a nutshell, I am an advisor and I enjoy working with and helping entrepreneurs who own family enterprises put their affairs in order by creating a Family Agreement. The phrase "put your affairs in order" is usually reserved for Doctors when they are telling patients they are going to die soon. This might explain why many owners avoid these conversations and spend even less time planning for this inevitable event. By creating a Family Agreement your family enterprise is more likely to continue to create wealth after you are gone and your important family relationships are not likely to be harmed in the process.

The aim of this book is to share with you as owners of family enterprises, and your professional advisors, the importance of creating a Family Agreement. I believe this approach to be a more practical and, dare I say, fun approach when compared to the more traditional model for dealing with the succession and estate planning issue; not an approach to be dreaded or avoided.

In survey after survey of owners of family enterprises, especially small to medium sized enterprises, owners have indicated that having a formal written succession plan is the most important tool towards a successful transition to the next generation. Yet, when over ten thousand of these same owners were asked in 2004 and again in 2006 by the Canadian Federation of Independent Businesses, less than 10 per cent said they had one.

This is consistent with my own observations working with owners of family enterprises over most of my career as an advisor. Here is what owners have told me:

The succession and estate planning process takes too much time and money and there is no guarantee of success. The process is complex and confusing and involves emotional risk dealing with family members on such issues as death, money, ownership and control. The process is driven by professional advisors who are too product and fee focused working independently of each other, who drive the process from their point of view and not the owner's point of view.

So what do over 90 per cent of owners do? Go back to their comfort zone running their family enterprise and do nothing on succession and estate planning issues as the survey indicated.

Why the Metronome Method? Have you ever tried to describe in 30 seconds or less what Succession and Estate Planning for a Family Enterprise means?

One of the challenges we as professional advisors have is what is sometimes called the Curse of Knowledge[1], resulting in technical jargon being used that very few people understand. Take, for example, the phrase succession and estate planning of a family enterprise. The phrase itself is long and the words within the phrase need explanation. The phrase and words mean different things to different people. For example, in the context of this book, succession is referring to ownership succession not necessarily who is going to run the business; family enterprise is referring to one family's controlling ownership in a portfolio of assets which typically includes the operating business, real estate, investment holding company, and philanthropic assets. The operating business may have been sold but the family enterprise can continue to create wealth over future generations.

The critical missing piece in the Succession and Estate plan is what I call a Family Agreement. The Metronome Method is a metaphor of how to create a Family Agreement so that the owner and her family can achieve the real goal which is to attain the peace of mind that the future is secure for the owner's family and the owner's family enterprise after his or her death.

The Metronome Method is based on the premise that every good thing starts with taking the first critical step. The first step primes the pump, so to speak, and significantly increases the odds that you

---

[1]   Chip Heath and Dan Heath, *Made to Stick;* Random House, 2007, p.20

will complete the task or achieve the goal. What is the goal? Is it the Succession and Estate Plan? Is it a change to your will or other legal agreements? These are all tools and activities to reach the ultimate goal. The ultimate goal is for you and your family to have peace of mind today that your affairs are in order after your death so that the future is secure for your family, family enterprise and important family relationships.

The process of creating a family agreement with all the stakeholder members within your family will help you identify and address potential issues when it comes to the ultimate transition of your family business at death. The Metronome Method® is focused on creating a family agreement for family owned businesses. However, the importance of creating a family agreement will work for anyone who has any wealth to transfer upon their death, not just to families that own businesses. I will share with you an approach to succession and estate planning for your family and family enterprise that will strengthen, not destroy, your business and enhance, not fracture, the relationships with the people you love the most. This approach is based on many years of experience gained from working with families who own substantial businesses and who struggle with the succession and estate planning issue. I will also share with you best practices from some of the world's most successful families and examples of succession and estate planning gone awry with prominent families in history.

I help owners of family enterprises and their families put their affairs in order so that when the owner dies the family enterprise continues to flourish and the family relationships remain strong and supportive. History has shown that when owners die and their family takes over the ownership of the business, in many cases it is a disaster.

The Problem: Death of Owner creates Liquidity and Harmony Crisis

A Family Agreement solves two important problems which oftentimes are created on the death of the owner/ founder of the family enterprise: A Liquidity crisis (need for cash) and a Harmony Crisis (disharmony among family members who previously loved each other). Life Insurance can help solve the Liquidity problem but not the Harmony problem. A Family Agreement can proactively solve the Harmony problem. You will learn how to create a Family Agreement throughout the book.

The Solution: The Metronome Method, a Musical Metaphor for the Family Agreement

The Metronome Method is a musical metaphor for the Family Agreement. A Metronome is an essential object that ensures practicing musicians stay in time and in tune with each other before the great performance. The Metronome is as important to practicing musicians for creating great music as a Family Agreement is essential to owners and their family members when planning the succession and estate plan for the family and the family business. The Family Agreement will prepare the surviving family members for their great performance as owners, many for the first time, when the owner/conductor leaves the stage forever. I bring the Metronome to family meetings I facilitate to remind everyone of the goal. That helps to make a fairly complicated, abstract, emotionally charged planning process concrete, simple to understand and positive. The main goal is for the owner and her family to collaborate, disagree respectfully, resolve differences, practice, share and create together a song or vision so that when the time comes after the owner's death, everyone knows their role and the music continues in the family and the business for many generations to come.

Creating a Direction and Framework for Legal Documents

Family Agreements are not legal documents and are not intended to replace important legal documents such as wills, buy/sell agreements, tax planning documents, life insurance policies or trusts. Family Agreements are intended to give direction and provide a framework so that legal documents which ultimately decide what happens to the largest family Asset (the Family Enterprise) upon the death of the owner and founder, reflect the wishes of the owner and his family as outlined in a well-rehearsed shared vision contained in the Family Agreement. History has shown that the world's most successful businesses that bucked the trend by surviving and flourishing well beyond the third generation had a family agreement (*They may have called it something else*). Conversely, the newspapers continue to be filled with stories of family members from some of the world's largest family owned businesses going to court to tear up the family enterprise and the relationships which were once strong and supportive.

Why Listen to Me?

I am a CA, Family Enterprise Advisor (FEA), and owner of the Canadian Succession Protection Company, a family business specializing in succession, estate planning and life Insurance solutions. I have spent a substantial portion of my life growing up with or helping family enterprises, gaining first-hand experience of what happens to the family and the family business at death. There are unique challenges and misconceptions that lead many business owners into a false sense of confidence that their affairs are in order. It is rare that there is a well thought-out and rehearsed succession and estate plan, and even rarer that the actual execution of an estate plan reflects the owner and founder's intentions.

These families clearly did not have a Family Agreement. There could be lots of insurance, a well-constructed will, a state of the art tax plan and even a complete succession and estate plan, and the family enterprise and the family relationships could still blow up following the death of the owner and founder.

When the Conductor Leaves the Stage

He or she is no longer there to act as the key leader of the family business and the family.

I call this leadership role the "conductor" (*borrowed from the world of music*) as a perfect metaphor for the role of owner /founder of a family enterprise attempting to create a succession and estate plan with the band members (family members) before she leaves the stage permanently. You will notice that, beginning with the title, I use a lot of musical metaphor throughout this book. I am an amateur musician who likes to perform with bands when I am not designing insurance solutions for estate plans or providing succession and estate planning advice to owners of family enterprises. Music in general, and an orchestral band in particular, or any musical group for that matter, has a leader who helps to get the best out of its members in terms of creating great music which will be played over and over again for many years. Creating music is also inspirational and fun requiring the ultimate collaboration and communication amongst each of the participants in the band. In fact, I am suggesting that this is not only a good metaphor for succession and estate planning but a great model for preparation of the first great performance which will be played out by those family members left behind when we exit the stage permanently.

The Largest Succession and Ownership Transfer in History

This subject of succession and estate planning for owners of family businesses is a hot topic today. A great deal of the financial wealth of the world was created and resides with family owned or controlled businesses.[2] Even conservative estimates indicate that upwards of 80 percent of the world's businesses are either owned or controlled by one family. It is estimated that $10 trillion of wealth will transition to subsequent generations over the next 10 years in the U.S and upwards of $1.3 trillion here in Canada. Because of these numbers there is no shortage of advice in this area.[3] The business book shelves are filled with advice to owners and their professional advisors on succession and estate planning, tax, will planning, insurance planning, retirement planning etc. However, there is very little empirical evidence that formalized succession and estate plans are being done and more importantly that they actually work. Anecdotally, many owners and their professional advisors would suggest they've benefitted from transition planning for that moment when the owner and founder are no longer there conducting the band. The traditional approach of advisors providing specialist advice and documents within their specific area of expertise (legal, tax, insurance, wealth management, accounting) exclusively to the owner in the confines of the "silo" and in isolation of each other and of most of the key family members, does not appear to be working. Many family enterprises, possibly the next world class company, appear to last only one or two generations and the triggering event often times is the death of the owner/founder.

---

[2]   Kelin E. Gersick, John A. Davis, Marion McCollom Hampton, Ivan Lansberg *Generation to Generation Life Cycles of the Family Business*, Harvard Business School Press, Boston 1997 Introduction Pg. 2.

[3]   Richard E. Jackim and Perry Phillips, *The $10 Trillion Opportunity*, Canadian Edition, A Guide for Professional Advisors, Exit Planning Institute 2007.

The purpose of this book is to provide an approach to succession and estate planning for Family Enterprises which can be fun and something to look forward to for the owner and family, rather than a process to be dreaded. The process is called the Metronome Method®. Early participation from the family is required and is done before we call in the technical experts to put the plan in place. We will think big, yet start small, drawing comparisons and stories from some of the world's biggest families—who typically began as a small one to two person family owned business. I suggest that the lessons learned from this book are more effective when the family members are young and the businesses are small to medium sized enterprises. Family owned businesses are most vulnerable when wealth is transferred from the first to the second generation. Creating a plan is only the beginning. All members of the band must rehearse this plan for that day when you leave the stage permanently. This gives a sense of urgency to the planning and provides more clarity to the process. There is no downside to do this type of planning. It will make your family business more valuable and your family closer as you begin to share the vision and prepare your family for ownership transition as stewards and not combatants. To that end, music continues to be created in your family, your family enterprise and your community for many generations.

Life Insurance Advisors bring a Sense of Urgency and Clarity to the Succession Process

An owner of a successful third generation family business once told me that he gets annoyed when life insurance people are talking about succession and estate planning, when all they really want to do is sell him the big policy and make lots of commission. This may be true, but a succession and estate plan without funding isn't much of a plan. The insurance professionals who work with clients who own family businesses are usually very well trained on succession and estate planning issues. More importantly, we are skilled in creating a sense of urgency and bringing these so called 'soft issues' to the forefront, knowing that life has a habit of throwing curve balls when least expected. Also, money cannot guarantee insurability or control the timing of your death. Owning a business and having substantial wealth does not give you a free pass. On the contrary, having wealth without preparing your family for ownership can cause your family enterprise and your loving family relationships to die with you.

ACKNOWLEDGEMENTS

I would first of all like to thank my wife Lynn and my son Grant for the many times I interrupted their lives asking for feedback on the chapters and for the green light to keep on going.

I would never have thought about writing a book if it was not for author, entrepreneur and marketing genius Bill Bishop of Bishop Communications Inc. Bill was also my senior editor. He not only provided encouragement but suggested I tell interesting stories and use metaphors to deliver the message. Thanks Bill.

I would like to thank Corey Kilmartin for the cover design and layout and Sonia Marques for coordinating with iUniverse. I would like to thank Ross Landers, CA, Partner, Green Landers, for taking the time in the middle of a large project to provide feedback on the book.

If you are trying to deliver a message to an audience it is really important that you get unfiltered feedback from that audience. In that regard, special thanks goes to Larry Smith, CEO of Kathbern Management, R. B. Cameron, CEO of Cameron Corporation, Jim Eisenhauer, CEO of ABCO Industries for providing excellent constructive feedback as owners of Family Enterprises and to Paul MacDonald, Executive Director of the Canadian Association of Family Enterprises(CAFE).

Finally, thanks to my parents Donald "D.J." and Theresa who taught me the fundamentals of life, family and business in a small country store where adversity was never far away.

CHAPTER ONE

EARLY LESSONS

The Fire

I learned at the age of seven what happens when you almost lose everything.

It was January 6, 1959. My family lived in a small town in Pictou County, Nova Scotia. We owned the general store that was, for the most part, the central meeting place for the town of Ardness. I had seven brothers and sisters at the time; Mom ran the store, while my Dad ran a lumber company. The store sold just about everything from soup to nails. It was the heart and soul of the community. Everyone would stop to chew the fat, while sitting on benches around the counter. Mom would have a pot of tea on the stove and fresh biscuits to pass around.

Our house was just across the street. It was a fairly modern new home with a big veranda and beautiful yard overlooking farm fields right through to the Northumberland Strait. Sitting on the veranda in the summer you could almost see the lobster fishermen pulling traps up into their boats.

But on that cold fateful day in January something happened that taught us a lesson we will never forget. Around two in the afternoon an electrical fire broke out in the stairwell, and quickly spread to the rest of the house. My teenage sister, Joan, happened to be home from school that day. She spotted the fire and went into action. She raced through the house and got everyone out, including my Mom and two babies. Coming home from school, as I approached our home, I saw my sister with the babies and my Mom without any coats on the coldest day of the year rushing towards the store which was just across the street from our family home. I could also see two men on the roof and thick black smoke streaming out of the upstairs windows.

First Important Lesson: You can always replace your stuff, but you can never replace your family

Over the rest of the day, we watched the fire completely consume our house and everything we owned, including family pictures, and most distressing to me at seven years old, all of my toys, especially my hydraulic truck. It is not possible for me to adequately communicate how I felt at the time, but surprisingly, I found the whole experience quite interesting. It was fascinating to watch all of our possessions go up in smoke, with kind of a dispassionate detachment. Looking back I realize that I felt this way because we did not lose our most important possession, which was our family. That's the lesson I learned, that you can lose every material possession you own, but if you have your family, it doesn't really matter. That's what my Dad said as he was doing a head count: "You can always replace your stuff, but you can never replace your family."

In the months and years following the great fire, our family weathered many other ups and downs. We actually ended up living in the store, and never rebuilt the family house across the street. In this way, our family and family business *(which had been in my father's family since the late 19th century)* became virtually one and the same. We were living right inside our business twenty-four/ seven.

Second Lesson: Pre-mature death of the owner triggers tough decisions for the family and the business

In March 1970, my Dad had a heart attack and died right there in the store while telling one of his famous stories to his friends. My Mom took over running the place and we helped her out. My Dad's lumber operations, including a saw mill and woodlands, which had supported the family for over half a century, were unfortunately liquidated at fire sale prices. Suddenly the store was responsible for generating all the money needed to support the family of nine kids, five of whom were still living at home. Just recently, as I write this book, my Mom passed away peacefully at the age of 91. She left behind nine grateful children and many fond memories for us to cherish. Sadly, though, the store, which had been in my father's family since the 1890's, is no longer in operation. My Mom closed it in 1993.

The Importance of being in time and in tune

Fortunately, through all of this, my siblings and I have stuck together. Although we all have different personalities and often disagree, there is a strong bond between us. We know that no matter what happens, on a basic level, we are all on the same page when it comes to family values especially when it comes to discussing issues such as money and family business. I call this being in time and in tune with each other.

I was able to experience the positive benefits of a Family Agreement when I acted as Executor of my Mom's estate which was distributed equally just a few years ago to nine siblings without any disagreement or conflict. The primary reason was that my Mom realized that death could come at any moment just like what happened to my Father and you must have your affairs in order and have those intentions communicated as a regular course of business at least once a year. This was a Family Agreement in action that provided certainty and guidance for many years to the family as to what will happen when the ultimate transfer of whatever wealth remains at death to all the beneficiaries.

These seminal experiences of my youth have an important impact on my work as a professional advisor to business owners and their families. I can relate to their struggles and aspirations for their companies and their families. I also know first-hand that the so-called dileneation between the business and the family is an artificial boundary. They are usually one and the same. That's why planning the future of a family business, including succession and estate issues, must address important relationship concerns and not just focus solely on the financial and legal agreements. Without incorporating this human element into the discussion, serious problems can disrupt the harmony of the family, and ultimately the fate of the business.

I've also observed that many entrepreneurs do not adequately prepare their family for the ownership transfer at death and do not take time to figure out who will own and control (not just run) their business after they die. That's because they don't talk about death, and they don't really think they are ever going to die. Many of them when asked will say that they care what happens to their business after they are gone, but their actions or inaction speaks differently and some owners simply believe that magically things will somehow work out. They don't realize that this attitude is going to really hurt their family, not just financially, but could destroy the family relationships that took a whole lifetime to build.

The Metronome Method®

If you want your family to stick together and carry on the success of your business, you need everyone to be in time and in tune. I use this phrase because I am also a musician. Music was very important in our family. We had a huge upright grand piano in our house, and someone was always playing it. Kids would come into the store, and head for the piano. My Dad could often be heard bashfully playing sweet waltzes on the fiddle near the piano. The wooden portable radio in the store was also always on, playing Scottish music for the local fisherman and farmers who were hanging around the store.

These days, I play the piano, tenor saxophone and accordion. I'm not a professional, but I enjoy playing with family and friends. Recently, I had an insight that there is a connection between my musical interests and my advisory work. For a long time, I've contended that the families are more successful if they are in time and in tune with each other. I realized that everyone needs something to keep generating good vibes or rythms. For musicians, this is accomplished by using a metronome. This device sets the tempo for a piece of music so that the musicians can stay in time. For practicing musicians, whether they are in a symphony orchestra, rock or jazz band, the metronome is an essential tool. It sets the rhythm and keeps everyone playing together at the same tempo. As in music, this coordination is very important in a family that owns a successful business. This kind of business is more than bricks and mortar. It is also about passion, feelings, and hopes and dreams. There is a lot of baggage and unspoken resentments that may go way back to childhood. They need a metronome too.

That's why I developed The Metronome Method®. It is a quick and fun way to secure the future of your family and your business. I emphasize quick because you don't want this kind of process dragging out over many years. It is essential to interact positively with your family and clear up any issues that are festering and this can even be a fun way to do it. The great part of this process is that it helps pull everything together once and for all so you can enjoy your life and prosper while running your business.

Taking the musical analogy further, the process helps you and your family stay on the same page of music.

We figure out:

1. What song you want to sing and have sung by others after you are gone
2. Write the sheet music
3. Turn on the metronome
4. Practice the song together with all the key members of the band.

After a few rehearsals, you and your family will be ready to perform on your own. Experience shows that this performance will be replayed over and over for many years, even if you change conductors.

Central to this model is what I call The Family Accord®. This is an important family agreement that is the missing piece in traditional succession and estate planning for family owned businesses. It describes and outlines the steps of what happens to your business and family when you are not there. This vision is the missing piece that provides the framework for everything else. It is the sheet music that each family member will sing from no matter who holds the baton.

This book was written as a professional approach to this subject. In each chapter, I will give you direction on what to do, and examples on how other families have done it. Think of it as a music school for your family succession and estate planning. You will take a few lessons, practice a few things, and learn how to make great music on your own. I will simply act as the metronome to keep you in tune and in time. Enjoy!

CHAPTER TWO

THE ROTHCHILDS AND
THE VANDERBILTS

Consider the Rothschilds and the Vanderbilts, two famous business families from history. If you go back to the 1800s, both of these families were titans of industry, one in Europe and one in America. The Rothchilds were Europe's bankers, and the Vanderbilts were the American transportation family, owning railroads and steamships. While they were both amongst the world's wealthiest families at the time, the long-term fate of these families could not be more different.

In 1973, the Vanderbilts had their first family reunion. You would have thought it would be a swanky affair, but in fact it was reported by Arthur Vanderbilt II "When 120 of the Commodore's descendants gathered at Vanderbilt University in 1973 for the first time, there was not a millionaire among them"[1]. This was not a particularly close family. They had only gotten together once in almost 100 years.

Across the ocean, the Rothschild story is a dramatic contrast. They continue to grow and flourish today as one of the world's wealthiest families. They have also stuck together through thick and thin.

---

[1]   Arthur T. Vanderbilt II, *Fortune's Children, the Fall of the House of Vanderbilt*: Harper 2001 (1st edition published in 1991) p. IX

How these two families dealt with inter-generational succession and the transfer of their money will be discussed in more detail later in this book. The important thing to realize at this point is that your business and your family are at cross-road like the Vanderbilts and the Rothchilds were at in the 1800s. You have to ask yourself, how do you want things to really work out?

CHAPTER THREE

IT'S NOT ALL ABOUT THE NUMBERS

You can't expect your family to play in time and in tune if you don't invite them to the practice sessions.

This is very common with small to medium-sized family-owned businesses. The owner/founder typically makes all the decisions, and the family is left out of the equation. This can result in a lot of acrimony in the family, and the demise of the company. There are hundreds of examples of this outcome.

The owner/founder often thinks they have done all the right things. They've met with their accountants, their lawyers, their life insurance person, and sometimes many other financial advisors. They've put together a plan to deal with the tax and legal issues involved in succession and estate planning. This gives them a false sense of comfort, an illusion that everything has been covered. But that's not usually the case.

Charlie's Story

Let's consider Charlie. He's 60 years old and has been operating his manufacturing firm for 30 years. He started it with $100 that he borrowed from his father. Now his company is worth $10 million. His son Tom is a key person in the business, and his daughter Lisa is going to university and works part-time in junior roles. He has another younger son, John, from his first marriage. John is a carpenter who builds cabinets.

Although Charlie knows he is the key person in the business, he has forgotten that he is running a family business, and that his family needs to be part of his planning. Charlie became acutely aware of this reality two years ago when he contemplated selling his business. Charlie met with his CA and had a valuation done of the business. That's when he learned that the company might fetch up to $10 million. Charlie was excited by this news, and began to dream of retiring to Florida with his wife Susan. He started to put the wheels in motion and entertained offers from potential buyers. He did all this without consulting his kids. He didn't even tell Susan.

Charlie realized later that he had made a huge mistake. Through the grapevine, his son Tom, who was the most senior employee in the company, heard about the impending sale. Outraged, Tom phoned his sister Lisa, and was shocked when she said "all businesses can be sold at any time without notice to anyone, including family." Lisa, for her part, wondered why Tom was so surprised.

Later that night, Charlie has a big blowout with Susan who was also angry that she had not been informed either. He was in the dog house for weeks.

Although Charlie's family had never been close, and had experienced some problems during the divorce and his subsequent marriage to Susan, they had always been cordial with each other. But now things went off the rails. It seemed like everyone was arguing with everyone else about the company, its assets, and what would happen if Charlie were to sell it, or if he were to die prematurely. It got so bad, that Charlie and Susan took off for Florida for Christmas because nobody wanted to come over for dinner.

Charlie had been making the sale of his business all about numbers. His CA, his lawyers, and other advisors, had done very little to dissuade Charlie of this idea. Although the accountant and other advisors had mentioned family dynamics, it was done in a cursory manner with little emphasis on doing anything substantive about it. They gave Charlie the notion that the family dynamics were "soft" issues and by implication less important issues and the money was the key to everything. It is like a fitness coach who gets you to do push-ups and cardio everyday and mentions off-hand that you should also watch your diet, but doesn't offer any further expertise or help on eating better.

Charlie put his plans to sell his business on hold indefinitely. His relationship with Tom is cordial, but a little frosty. His daughter Lisa no longer works at the company because she said it's not fun anymore. Two of the key employees quit and went to work for the competition, and to top if off, his accountant told him that his business valuation has dropped by two or three million. Now the bank, which has a covenant on some of the company's assets, has called Charlie in for a meeting. Moreover, his son John, the cabinet-maker put a call through his lawyer, who sent Charlie a letter demanding to see the financial statements for the company.

Charlie's story, which is a composite of many families we have all read about or encountered over the years, is very common. Obviously, if Charlie were to do it all again, he would take a different route. He would bring the family into the discussion, and work towards a shared vision for what happens to the business and all of the assets when he is no longer owning and operating the company.

The Immortality Trap

Another typical problem with human beings is that we logically know that we are going to die, but emotionally we really don't think it is going to happen to us any time soon. I call this affliction the Immortality Trap. As a result, we don't do enough to prepare our family for our inevitable demise. It goes without saying that having an up-date will and adequate life insurance are minimum requirements to ensure our affairs are in order for the owner of a family business. However, if you are the owner and founder of the family enterprise, more advanced planning is required which focuses not just on the numbers but the important family relationships. This lack of planning can create chaos for the family, the business, the employees, and everyone else in the community who depends on that business.

Some business owners tell me that this problem does not relate to them because they are planning to sell the business. Obviously, they haven't talked to Charlie. Even so, their logic is wrong because even if they sell the operating business, they still have a family enterprise consisting of a portfolio of assets which may include real estate, philanthropic assets and wealth from the original operating business sitting in assets or an investment company which will need to be divided and allocated between your family members, Canada Revenue Agency and or a charity. They are also making the assumption that the sale of their business will happen before they die, in a perfect sequence. We all know that life doesn't happen that way.

People are also prone to procrastination, especially when it comes to subjects related to death. Our fear of death is masked by a complacency bordering on denial. There is no sense of urgency to get this work done today, so it often never gets done at all. As a result, owners delay connecting and communicating with their family about all of these important issues, until it is too late. It is sad to see people in their 70s and 80s trying to connect with their adult children with whom they have not had a great relationship in the past. It may be too late.

There is also the fear of stirring the pot, and unleashing repressed emotion and resentments. This is understandable. When there is an elephant in the room, it is sometime easier just to ignore it and hope it will go away. You may think that this only applies to small and unsophisticated business owners and their families. But this also happens in some of the largest family businesses in the world. The same issues, dynamics, and problems apply to the largest companies, and for the most part, the problems are even bigger and more devastating because the stakes are higher. I will give you some examples of this later in the book.

So hopefully you now see that is not all about numbers. The numbers are very important, but the family can be as important or depending on what you value, much more important, and ironically by ignoring the family element it can have a cataclysmic impact on the numbers.

So don't end up like Charlie, or the thousand of other similar victims, whose family businesses have disappeared from the face of the earth. Thankfully, there is a better road to take. In the next chapter, we will talk about the value of having a Family Agreement and how it can help your family and your business stay in time and in tune, and increase the odds that the family will not blow up but rather continue to grow and flourish as a family and a business when the owner/founder has left the stage.

CHAPTER FOUR

THE FAMILY AGREEMENT

The King Lear Plan

If King Lear had made a family agreement, his story would not have been a tragedy. As you may recall from your high school English classes, Shakespeare's King Lear handed over the reins of his kingdom to his three daughters. This transfer of power was done capriciously and without a lot of forethought. Within a short while, Lear was out on his ear, and his children had made a debacle of his empire.

Sadly, King Lear's story is not a fantasy, but a reality in many family enterprises today. The king of the castle, the person who started the business and built it up from nothing, often makes a fatal mistake by not planning ahead for succession. This planning is critical because in a family enterprise it is not just about finding a new King or President, it is about selecting new owners. These new owners will likely, but not necessarily, be family members.

It is also important that, once you have decided that a family agreement is important to you, that you follow a proper process. It is not just about having lunch with your kids, and over a few beers, blurt out your strategic plan for the family enterprise. In these kinds of meetings, the patriarch or matriarch holds court, while the simpering offspring hold their tongues and seethe with resentment.

Lessons from the Godfather Movie

I'm sure you're aware of or heard about the Godfather movies. It is a modern day Shakespearean tragedy about a "family" enterprise. Vito Corleone (Marlon Brando) is the founder of the business. He knows what it takes to run such an enterprise, but his kids (Michael, Sonny, Fredo, and Connie), have grown up in a bubble, enjoying the benefits of his hard, albeit illegal work. The Godfather doesn't spend any time thinking about his demise, or really communicating a succession plan to his family. He acts as if he is immortal. As well, Sonny, being the oldest, is under the assumption that he will become the new Godfather because he is helping his father run the business. Meanwhile, Michael is trying to go straight, and says he doesn't want to have anything to do with the family business. Fredo is kind of pathetic, and no one really knows what to do with him. As for Connie, it is just assumed that she will marry and have babies.

If you've seen the movies, you will know that everything goes off the rails when the Godfather is shot and eventually dies. Sonny turns out to be a terrible leader because he is so hot headed, and doesn't think strategically. His enemies were able to manipulate him and he dies in a hail of machine gun bullets. Surprisingly to everyone, Michael decides to take over, and turns out to be a ruthless gangster like his father, as well as a brilliant strategist. Unfortunately, Fredo betrays Michael, who has him assassinated; a metaphor for the litigation that many family members have with their siblings who once loved each other and then feel betrayed. If you remember, at the end of the third movie, Michael is all alone, abandoned by his wife and family, and dies a solitary death, thereby ending the family enterprise known as the Corleone family.

You can dismiss the Godfather as simply an action-packed Mafia movie, or you can see it as a lesson in the perils of a family enterprise without a plan. If the Godfather had taken some time to communicate his wishes to his four kids, and recognized that every family member is a stakeholder in the family enterprise, things might have turned out much better. It is not about reaching some perfect agreement and consensus among everyone, so that everyone is super happy, it is about reaching an agreement on what's going to happen, and how it will impact each person as a stakeholder. In other words, they might not like it, but at least they have had a chance to voice their opinion, and in the end, they know what to expect.

It is the uncertainty of not knowing what will happen that causes all of the problems. This means that people are building their expectations around something that might not happen, or they react with shock, anger, and resentment, when it doesn't turn out the way they expected. In other words, it is better that a child realizes they won't be getting any money, or any ownership in the family business, than find out about it at a will reading. This kind of shock can tear the family apart forever.

In Dickens' novel *Bleak House*, many generations have been waiting for the resolution of a huge estate called Jarndyce versus Jarndyce. Because there are several versions of the will, and none is conclusive, the estate has been bound up in the courts for over 100 years. Meanwhile, all of the potential beneficiaries have been waiting and hoping to get the money. This has caused people to commit suicide, forego a career, and engage in running battles with other family members. The ultimate irony is, that once the estate was finally settled, it was worth nothing, because all of the lawyer fees ate it up. It is the ultimate cautionary tale of an estate without a family agreement.

If you don't want to end up like King Lear, The Godfather, or the Jarndyce family, you need to create a family agreement. Therefore the question is: What is a family agreement, and how do you make one?

Visualizing Your Family Agreement in Action after your Death

The first step is to honestly imagine what would happen to your business and your family had you died last night. So think about it. You are now dead. Magically you can see what's going on, but you have no voice. What is happening? What is your spouse dealing with? What are your kids thinking? What are they talking about? Who are they calling for help and advice? What's going on at the office? What are the clients, customers and suppliers thinking and doing? What are the bankers doing? What does your will (*your last voice*) say? Where are the records, passwords, keys to the files? Who is the Executor (Trustee) for the business? For your personal assets?

This is a visualization process of trying to imagine if you did a good job of putting your affairs in order or not. At the very least you have begun a conversation with your spouse and your family members and that is a good thing. You simply have to take that first step of doing it. The first time we do it we realize very quickly that we had not left our house in order. While we thought we were doing a good thing by simply building up this great business, if our planning stopped there, we may have actually left our family with a huge problem. We actually created turmoil for the people we love the most by not preparing them for the ownership transfer and by not seeking their input or at least having a conversation about your plans.

It is important to realize that simply having a will and some life insurance does not guarantee that everything post-you would be blissful. A will and insurance is just a minimum requirement because it does not address many important issues that need to be communicated and dealt with.

I've found that when a business owner does this kind of crash-test, they wake up to the bigger problem at hand, and now see the necessity of a family agreement. It is kind of like Scrooge waking up on Christmas and realizing the folly of his ways, and eventually he is glad that he was visited by the three ghosts.

Secondly, you need to create a vision of what you want to have happen. To develop the vision, ask yourself questions like these:

- Who do you want to own and control your shares in your family enterprise when you are not there?
- Who is your named successor to operate and run your business?
- Do you want ownership concentrated in one individual family member or have a sibling partnership?
- What happens to other family members who are not involved in the business?
- What role, if any, do other family members not involved in the operating business wish to play in the family enterprise?

Sometimes the most important insight at this point is that you don't have any answers to these questions. This is a wake up call because you can now clearly see the turmoil that could ensue. The odd person simply just doesn't care. They say that things will work out, and who cares anyway because they are dead. That's why this process is not for everyone. You have to really care about your family and your business, and about the legacy that you leave behind. Do you want your family to think fondly of you when you are gone, or curse your very memory?

Starting to formulate your vision is a great first step. It wires your brain to look at your situation more closely, and make better decisions. For example, you might realize that you should pull a King Lear and create a sibling partnership between your three daughters. Or you will realize that Michael should run the family business because Sonny is too impetuous, and that it is probably not a good idea to send Fredo to Las Vegas to run a casino. You might also realize that your succession and estate planning is so ambiguous that your assets may be tied up in the courts for a century or more.

Conversely, Family enterprise succession can be a very positive experience. You will realize that by taking a few simple steps, your family enterprise can continue to prosper for generations and that inevitable family conflict can be resolved through a well defined process of respect and good communication. This process will increase the possibility that your memory and good work will be cherished.

That's why I enjoy working with family enterprises. They are the backbone of our economy. They outperform other kinds of companies by almost any financial metric.[1] Ultimately, a family agreement is about confidence. Once in place, you have the confidence that your family and your business will be okay after you are gone. This kind of confidence is invaluable.

So begin by imagining the day after your demise, and create the vision by answering the key questions. Doing this, you will begin to write the notes and lyrics to your Succession and Estate song in your songbook. The next step will be to communicate with your family and put together the band that will finish the composition, and then rehearse and perform this great piece of music together before it is too late.

---

[1]   Danny Miller and Isabelle LeBreton Miller, *Managing for the Long Run: Lessons in Competitive Advantage from Great Family Businesses* (Boston Harvard Business Press Books, 2005), p.14-15

CHAPTER FIVE

THE METRONOME METHOD

What would happen if you died today? What would happen to your business? What would happen to your family? What would happen to other stakeholders, such as your employees?

Most business owners have never answered these questions. They think they have because they've got a will, some insurance, and have done some tax and estate planning. They've missed the key ingredient, a family agreement. As a result what might happen the day after you die might not be what you really want.

The family agreement is like a metronome. It helps keep everything and everyone in time and in tune. Without a metronome, all the members of a band can be out of sync, causing tension and disharmony. As well, because the musicians haven't practiced together, the actual performance will not meet anyone's expectations.

That's why I developed a process called The Metronome Method®. It is a simple step-by-step approach you can use to get all of your performers in sync, in time, and in tune, to create beautiful music. The objective is to get everyone so rehearsed and in harmony that the performance can happen without you the conductor.

The Metronome Method has four stages:

1. Assess situation
2. Develop a shared Family Vision
3. Communicate
4. Create a Family Agreement

First Step: Assess Gap between What You Want to have Happen versus What Will Likely Happen

The first step in creating a family agreement involves assessing where you are at this moment in your succession and estate planning and comparing that to your vision of where you want it to be. A good place to start is to identify who are your stakeholders in your family enterprise.

Identify the Stakeholders

The Metronome Method is based on the fact that every family enterprise has many stakeholders having different roles and perspectives. This is illustrated by a three-circle model developed by Taqiuri and Davis in 1982 referred to in Exhibit 1. The three circles are family members, owners, and employees (including management), representing the three primary roles. The three circles are also interconnected demonstrating that some people are stakeholders in more than one circle. There are only seven different positions or roles that an individual stakeholder can occupy within the three circles.

For example, someone could be both a family member and an employee, or an employee and an owner, but not a family member. The founder of the company is typically a stakeholder in all three circles (owner, family member, and management employee) and this is indicated by position number seven in the model on Exhibit 1. This creates unique family dynamics regarding relationships between different people with different roles, perspectives, and agendas. That's why not having everyone on the same page, singing the same song, could be calamitous. It only takes one or two disgruntled stakeholders to bring down the whole enterprise because there was no family agreement.

Death of Owner of Major Hotel Chain triggers Disharmony

For example, in a well-publicized case (which I will disclose the identity of in a later chapter), a teenage niece of an owner/founder, who received by any measure a huge amount of wealth when the owner/founder died, decided that it was not enough, and tied the company up in litigation for many years. The legal battle and the diffusion it created in running the company, led to a forced sale of significant family holdings at a big discount. This was a major hotel chain that was extremely successful over a number of generations. This horror story happened even though the owner/founder thought he had done all of the necessary planning. But he hadn't included the family in the process. They didn't know what song to sing, they didn't have the notes, and they had never rehearsed or tried out the song together. In other words, they didn't have a metronome to keep them in time and tune.

That's why the first step is to assess the current situation. Ask yourself: "What will actually happen after I am gone?" You don't answer by reading your will or thinking of it from your point of view. The hotel owner/founder did that and was completely wrong about what happened. Instead, you need to look at the situation from the point of view of each stakeholder, and this requires a certain amount of empathy. It will also probably take you out of your comfort zone. This is why the Three Circles is a great tool. You simply identify each stakeholder and plot them into one of seven possible categories within the three circles (See Exhibit1). This will help you and members of your family, who currently are, or will, most likely become owners after your death clearly see what role each stakeholder plays within the Family Enterprise. More importantly, it identifies the stakeholders and how they perceive themselves and their roles within the Family Enterprise. The Three Circle model is a brilliant tool for Succession and Estate planning as a picture is worth a thousand words and provides everyone with greater insight into how they might feel, react and behave in the real performance (which happens during the reading of the will and afterwards). A clear objective analysis can predict what might happen. Typically, it reveals that your original expectations will not be met. You can accept this, or do something about it.

Second Step: Create a Shared Vision with Your Family

That's why the second step (Vision) is so important. You need to spend the time to plot out what you really want to have happen. Here is an example: You are the owner of a business, and you got hit by a truck last night. Now that you are dead, you want your business successor to be your son who is currently driving the business. You want him to own and control the business. That will happen through a buy-sell agreement. Your son will buy a majority ownership in the shares from your spouse, who inherited your shares, at a pre-determined formula for price valuation. The formula for valuation has already been well communicated to the family, and is included in the family agreement. In his book *Every Family's Business,* Dr. Tom Deans says that "when a child has his own money in the game they will honestly appraise the business"[1]. This son may have to borrow the money from the family bank by preparing a business plan or get some outside financing. Your other two children, who are not actively involved in the business, will receive

---

[1]   Thomas William Deans, *Every Family's Business*: Détente Financial Corporation, 2008, p. 96-97

an equalization payment from life insurance and other assets and possibly a minority ownership position in the business. Your son will continue to work in the business while holding a controlling ownership based on merit. The family will also continue to meet twice a year as a family council where issues such as governance, communication and succession are communicated to and from the other two circles of ownership and Business. The business will continue to be operated in an ethical manner. The family owners, including who is leading the business, may decide to recommend to the Board that outside professional managers be recruited to run the business, if no family member can be found or is interested in the role. The family business will also be run as a meritocracy as set out in the mission values statement. The purpose of the family meetings is to communicate to family members who are owners and non-owners what is happening in the family business, and how it affects them as stakeholders. It also gives opportunity for family members to play some role in the family enterprise and to voice their opinion.

This is one example of the detailed type of vision you need to create. Some people think this kind of planning is a soft issue that's not as important as tax planning and creating more wealth. But, as history has shown, it is the lack of a written and communicated shared vision that can cause huge problems in the family, including the total loss of the family's wealth. That's why we are adamant about taking this step. It cannot be glossed over. Otherwise, all of your good intentions and hard work will be for naught. It is also a very positive undertaking because it gives you the opportunity to develop a strategy to deal with your family at family gatherings where family members most certainly have unanswered questions. The most important one is what happens to your family enterprise and your family when you are not there? You have to deal with your family and these unanswered questions anyway, so it might as well be a positive experience.

Ask Four Powerful Questions to build a Shared Vision

Once you have identified who the stakeholders are in a Family Enterprise ask four powerful open ended questions from each stakeholder including the owner and spouse to identify potential issues and to give some direction as to what role, if any, individual family members wish to play when you the owner have exited the stage (*To find the four questions please go to How to Get Started on Your Family Agreement at the end of the book*). Typically, founding owners are surprised by family member's points of view on the family enterprise. The exercise of asking and receiving without judgment what people have to say is a very powerful collaboration exercise that will help to build consensus amongst families who up to now may have remained silent.

Third Step: Communicate the Vision with Regular Meetings to work on the Family Binder

Family communication is the third stage of the process. This is also the step that many business owners dread and shy away from because they are afraid to open up the Pandora's Box. They are afraid to disclose their wishes to their children because they may be perceived as playing favorites or as unfair if one of the children is given more than the others. The kids might lose motivation to pursue their own dreams if they know they will be given a lot of wealth. Controlling business owners are also used to holding their cards close to their vest, and not telling everyone what they are doing in the business.

While these hesitations are understandable, it is not wise to let them stop you from doing the right thing. If you really want your family to know how to carry your business forward after you are gone, you need to do something. Depending on your wishes, your family needs to know how to act as an owner, how to act as stewards of the family wealth, and if necessary, how to run the operations of the business. Remember, when you are gone, your family will most likely own your corporation. After your demise, the musicians will have to become the conductors. So if you are really serious about empowering your family, you need to communicate.

We have learned that creating a family enterprise binder together as a family is a good way to communicate with your family. This binder is like a manual that your family will follow when you are gone. For example, the binder explains who will own the shares in the company—the spouse, the children running the business, or children not involved in the business? Who gets the ownership control of the business? Is there a buy /sell agreement? Do the siblings just receive the shares, or do they need to buy them? How do deal with potential claims on the assets of the company by siblings who feel disinherited?

The binder also explains how the spouse will be provided for outside of the business. Is there life insurance in place to provide enough liquidity to the spouse? What income will be available for the spouse, and from where? Does the spouse own all the shares in the company? Do the children own any shares through a trust? What should the spouse do with the shares? Putting the answers to these questions in a binder gives direction to the family members and their advisors when you are not there.

It is better to create this binder first before adjusting your legal documents such as a will or a buy/sell agreement. Once you have your vision, and have written your directions, the content of the legal documents will be easier to create. It is like you have a song in your head, and now you want to communicate to the other members of the band what's in your head. You do that by writing down the name of the song, what musical key it is in, the speed of the song, the chord changes, and finally you put the melody and notes together. This sheet music helps you get the other members of the band to play the song with you.

In the best case scenario, the band helps you create the music. You can either write it all yourself and get the band to play, or you can have them collaborate on the creation of the song. Collaboration makes great music.

That's why we recommend you involve your family in the creation of your binder, so that it is truly a family agreement. This involves having a meeting with family members and other stakeholders as you are putting pen to paper, and writing your directions to them. In this way, there is much more buy-in because the affected parties have contributed to the creation of the agreement.

While it might seem daunting to include family members in this collaboration, and to divulge a lot of personal and confidential information, you must remember that your family will ultimately become involved at the reading of the will. That moment can either be the beginning of a great future for your family, or the beginning of a dissolution process.

If you give everyone an opportunity to participate in the process, they can't complain if they choose not to participate. They had the chance, and they will appreciate that. In other words, it is not necessary to have every member play along if it is not possible, but they should be given the opportunity and communicated to.

Of course, every family is different, with a multitude of unique relationship situations. That's why you need to determine your own best process for this project. There is no cookie-cutter approach. However, the principles of collaboration, sharing, dialogue and good communication are important to keep in mind.

Fourth Step: The Family Agreement

The fourth stage is your Family Agreement. This is the culminating document in a binder that outlines your wishes and your direction to the family. Whenever the family needs to make a decision or resolve a dispute, they will reference this family agreement. It will give a process to follow, and explain the principles of that process so that your family and your family enterprise will continue to grow and flourish. For a picture of what a family agreement might look like go to How to Get Started on Your Family Agreement at the end of the chapters in the book.

Exhibit 1

The Three Circle Model

Who are the stakeholders and how do they perceive their role within the Family Enterprise?

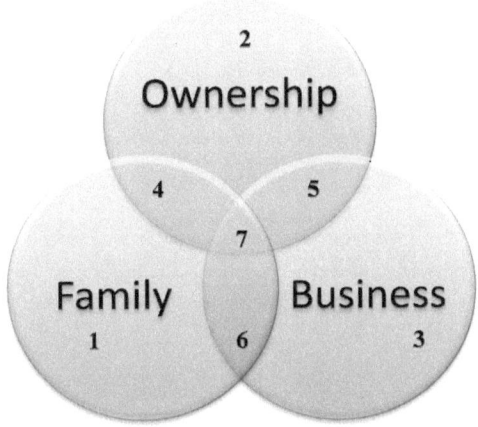

1. Family Members who are not actively involved in the business either as employees or owners.
2. External Investors who own part of the business but who do not work in it and are not members of the family.
3. Non-Family management and employees with no ownership.
4. Family Members who own shares in the business but who are not employees.
5. Owners who work in the business but who are not family members.
6. Family members who work in the business but who do not own shares.
7. Inhabiting all three circles are owners who are also family members and who work in the business.

Source: Adapted from R. Tagiuri and John A. Davis (1982) Bivalent Attributes of the Family Firm, reprinted (1996) in the Classics section of Family Business Review, Volume IX, Number 2, Summer, 199-208. Used with permission from Family Business Review, Sage Publications.

CHAPTER SIX

KEEPING THE SONGBOOK SIMPLE

When you are creating your family agreement, remember that you are not creating a Mozart opera. Think of it as the simple song you hear on the radio, with a few catchy lines sung over and over again. It is more like a pop song. It isn't as complicated to do as you might think. The most important step is to create the song with your family, and rehearse it a few times. This can be done in just a few meetings.

The Binder is The Family Songbook

To keep everything organized, we recommend you create the family song book. It is kind of like a family album. By creating this family song book, it makes the whole process more positive and fun and takes abstract ideas such as a shared vision and makes it concrete. Everyone has a role to play and a voice in singing the song. As the songwriter (business owner), you might create the song yourself or with your spouse, as a starting point. Your family can then help polish up the song by providing feedback, but everyone participates in the rehearsals.

The song book is a simple binder with some tabs in it. As you put together various components of the family agreement, you put them into the binder. This includes a vision statement of what you want to have happen to the family enterprise and the family when you are not there. This vision is written in plain everyday language. It is not a legalese document like a will. (*Note: This plain language vision is an excellent tool to give lawyers and accountants later to build the legal and tax agreements because they have something to work with. As the family song that has already been rehearsed, the work done by your advisors will be more in line with what you want. It will also save them time, which will save you money.*) Unfortunately, in far too many situations this process of building the vision first and then giving the vision to the professional advisors second is done in the reverse sequence. The legal and tax agreements are prepared first by the professional advisors working in their professional silos without ever consulting the other specialists and without a well thought out shared vision from the owner and her family. Can you imagine for a moment having a new house built and allowing the carpenters, the plumbers, the electricians, starting construction on your dream home without an architect's design or some blueprint (which you and your spouse have agreed upon) which represents in plain language what your new house will look like?

Some of the most successful families and family businesses in the world have gone through this process. They have beaten the odds, and have survived for multiple generations after the original founder died. This was not by accident. One of the reasons for this success is that there was regular two way communication between the business and the family and a process in place to communicate with each other while the founder was still alive. They established a protocol of good and frequent communication between the family, the ownership group, and the business.

Communicating the Vision through Regular Family Meetings: Lessons from Sam Walton

Sam Walton, the founder of Walmart, insisted that the family get together regularly to communicate with each other. By all accounts, this is still happening, even after Sam Walton died in 1992. The results speak for themselves. Walmart is the largest and most successful family enterprise in the world, with assets of more than $90 billion.

We can only speculate but one of the advantages of these family meetings was Sam's ability to instill, for example, a value of frugality. It is hard to imagine that a family worth $90 billion would need to be frugal, but that is the foundation of their success. It is rumored that up to the day he died, Mr. Walton drove his own half-ton truck. He didn't have chauffeurs and all of the other accoutrements of wealth. He was really a regular guy. He didn't have a sense of entitlement. He knew that you had to earn your keep and he was adamant about passing this lesson on to his family.

As in the case of Sam Walton, communicating your values is one major benefit of regular family meetings.[1] Of course, there is no guarantee that the next generation will observe, but in the case of the Walton family, it appears that it did. Making the attempt is better than doing nothing. Obviously, this kind of values-based communication must be done with some skill because no one, especially adult children, likes to be lectured on their values. The sooner you do this the better. Research shows that family businesses that have prospered for many generations took an early proactive approach. They established a set of rules or principles, and they communicated these at every opportunity. Family meetings are a core component of this approach, but face to face family meetings are not the only venue for communication in today's internet world of instant messaging.

The key is to simplify what you are trying to communicate. If you say too much in a rambling incoherent way, nothing will stick in their mind. So be clear about the simple message you want to

---

[1]   Bob Ortega, *In Sam We Trust*: Three Rivers Press, 2000 (Originally published in 1998) p.11

convey, and keep saying it over and over again. For example, you might want to instill a value of probity, which means goodness and decency. While your children might think the business is all about making money, and getting richer, you may be operating from a totally different perspective. You might see the role of the business as doing the right thing for all stakeholders involved; owners, family, employees, community. The financial success of the company is important, but doing the right thing is even more important. Communicating this once won't work; it should be shared over and over again, and demonstrated through action. In time, your children will copy what you do.

The very act of having family meetings is to demonstrate the importance of these intangible values. If the whole discussion revolves around taxes, trusts, dividends, shareholder agreement, and buy-sell agreements, your family might conclude that it is all about money. That's when greed sets in, and the next generation becomes mired in legal battles by lining up their own lawyers. This is not an idle fear; this outcome is being played out everyday in courtrooms around the world.

If you take a proactive approach to communication, your family could continue to work together positively for many generations. Recently, I attended a presentation by a man who was the fourth generation descendant of one of North America's wealthiest families with roots from the 19th Century. Today, there are more than 40 cousins and in-laws, who are all directly related to each other. To this day, they still communicate with each other, with open disclosure, within a governance structure. While the original operating company no longer exists, the wealth continues to create more wealth.

This structure of communicating vision, values, and rules, along with family meetings, puts everyone on the same page, singing the same song. The structure acts as the metronome, beating out the time and rhythm. The family can be as creative as they want to be, but there is an underlying structure of consistency and collaboration. This metronome method keeps it simple and fun, while allowing for each individual to have their say, and express their individual creativity.

Step one is to put together the binder. This will get you started, and act as a reminder that you are working on this project. Better to start slowly and maintain some consistency, than to start with a big flurry of activity, and then lose interest and abandon the effort. We want this kind of family communication to become an ingrained habit that continues forever.

Remember, the purpose of this binder to lay out what should happen to your family and your business when you are no longer there conducting the band. This exercise primes the pump. If you can get the family agreement done, you will have achieved the first critical step in preparing your succession and estate plan, which is to prepare your family to take over responsibility for ownership of the business. The family agreement is just one step in a much larger process, but it is a Foundation upon which all of the other components rely.

Create the Family Agreement Before you meet with the Lawyers and Accountants

One important point to emphasize: Doing the family agreement during a series of family meetings should happen before you meet with your lawyers, accountants and other advisors. You need to write the song, and rehearse the music with the band members, and the supporting cast, before you go into the recording studio.

Otherwise, you will spend a fortune trying to work out the tune, while the recording technicians are sitting doing nothing at $500 an hour. If you are fully prepared for the recording session, it will all go much smoother and quicker. It is even more important that you practice as a family, because you will not be there to lead the band when the show begins.

This might sound like having a root canal, but there are many payoffs, some of them immediate. By having the family meetings, and giving everyone a voice, the family will immediately become more united. There might be some disagreements to resolve, and can be unpleasant, but they have been aired and discussed. These disagreements can be resolved, and the family becomes even more united.

The key is to focus on the ultimate benefit, which is to keep your business together, while keeping your family united.

It is also helpful to make it fun. For example, you could ask each person to select their favorite family picture, perhaps a family celebration or wedding. They then pick a song title or piece of music that captures the spirit of the picture and bring this picture to the meeting with the song playing in the background. This exercise helps answer the important question: What's more important, your family or your business?

If the answer is that your family is most important, the second question is: Have you made sure that your business won't wreck your family? And the third question is: Have you made sure that your family won't wreck your business?

If you remain focused on answering these questions, you will naturally keep it simple.

CHAPTER SEVEN

LIQUIDITY AND HARMONY

When the owner and founder of the family business dies, there is a very high probability that two potential problems will be created for the business and the family: A Liquidity problem and a Harmony problem. Many financial advisors to family business focus on the liquidity issue. This is extremely important because your family will need cash when the owner (conductor) of the business is no longer there or dies. There may be debt to be repaid, or income taxes, or loss of company value because the key person is gone. Most of the time, the liquidity is addressed by life insurance if the owner has good health. It is a great liquidity tool because the death benefit ("cash") is created when it is needed, while the investment in premiums is a low drain on present or future capital. That's why we have provided life insurance to many of our clients for their estate plans. Life Insurance proceeds continue to be tax free in Canada. That is another compelling reason which makes life insurance attractive from an investment point of view.

However, I have also learned that liquidity is not enough. You can have liquidity, but no harmony. Often when the business owner dies, it triggers disharmony in the family, even if the family relationships were harmonious up to that point. All the life insurance in the world will not solve this problem. If no plan has been made and communicated, if no family agreement has been forged, then the family could be thrown into disarray. Who will take over the operation of the company? Who are the shareholders?

What happens to the children who already have positions in the operations of the business, compared to the family members who are not in the business? The spouse, who never had anything to do with the business, suddenly owns and controls all the shares? These scenarios and many others are recipes for family disharmony, potential litigation, and the demise of the business and the family.

Why does this happen? There are many reasons for this. One of the main reasons is that the spouse and the children have not been privy to this information up to this point and as a result had no voice in the outcome. Now they may be thrust into a position of being a beneficiary of shares, financial wealth or a position of responsibility in the family business that they do not perceive as fair or what they want. This is particularly problematic when the spouse inherits all the shares of the operating company or investment company which generally represents most of the wealth for the family (By *the way, many accountants set it up this way to defer tax*). The spouse who has never been actively involved in any of the decisions now is thrust into a situation where he or she is not prepared for ownership and the responsibility of owning and running a business and allocating shares and assets to the siblings.

Rothschilds and Vanderbilts Revisited

Remember the Rothschilds and the Vanderbilts from chapter two? They were two of the world's most famous business families at the time. While both families were founded by ambitious and far-sighted visionaries, their ultimate fates could not be more different.

Family empires were founded in the 1800s, The Rothschilds in Europe, and the Vanderbilts in the United States. The Rothschilds were known as the bankers of Europe, and the Vanderbilts were transportation barons in America, mostly railroads and steam ships. Both families amassed at the time the world's largest fortunes.

Today, many generations later, the Rothschilds are still considered one of the world's wealthiest families, with business interests around the globe. No one really knows their true financial wealth. Conversely, the Vanderbilts, while their name is very recognizable, are no longer a player in world business affairs. In fact, as I noted earlier in the book, the family had a reunion in 1973, the first reunion in almost a hundred years. Surprisingly, there was apparently not one millionaire among them at the time.

What was the difference between the Rothschilds, and the Vanderbilts? When Mayer Amschel Rothschild died, the family had a plan for both liquidity and harmony. But Cornelius (the Commodore) Vanderbilt appeared to focus only on liquidity. As a result, the next generation of Vanderbilts, didn't know what to do, and started bickering among each other, suing each other, leading to the biggest destruction of wealth in history. By contrast, Mayer Amshel Rothschild's plan for "Family Unity" at all costs, helped the next generation build on the fortunes of the founder. He was reported to have said on his deathbed to his eldest son in 1812 "Keep your brothers together and you will become the richest people in Germany".[1] They were imbued with a stewardship attitude, rather than an entitlement attitude. The Rothschild family established certain rules, principles, and structures with the primary intention to foster harmony and unity. In effect, a family agreement based on Partnership[2] interests for his five sons resembling a Family Bank was created. This agreement stipulated, for example, that if a family wanted money they had to come to the family bank and make an application. They had to justify why they wanted to borrow the

---

[1]   Niall Furguson, The House of Rothschild: The World's Banker, 1849-1999; Preface, p. xxii

[2]   Niall Furguson, The House of Rothschild: The World's Banker, 1849-1999; Preface, p. xxv

money, how they were going to pay it back, and it was to be used to improve the overall fortunes of the family and the business. There was no free lunch. Secondly, the family members were required to meet at least once a year to talk about the family and the business. Thirdly, if someone in the family had a good idea, they were obliged to share it with the rest of the family. Over the years, this family agreement has held everything together, and allowed the family to continue to grow and flourish. [3]

Of course, you might think that your family is not the Vanderbilts or the Rothschilds. You might think that their situation was more complicated, or that your family is not at risk. We have learned that every family business has hidden issues that often don't come to light until it is too late (That may explain why many business owners don't deal with this issue). This is unfortunate because it is not just the fate of your business that is at stake, but also the fate of your family. This will be exponentially exaggerated as the family grows and there are more stakeholders in the game (such as spouses, cousins, or siblings) the family may not have considered which can cause unforeseen issues to appear out of no where.

Unfortunately, the focus on liquidity is also a problem if it is considered to be the answer to the whole problem. The notion is that lots of money will solve all of the problems including bad planning. For example, you might imagine that a family member who receives millions and millions of dollars would be happy and feel harmonious toward the family. But sadly, this is not always the case.

---

[3]   James E. Hughes Jr., Family Wealth: Keeping it in the Family(Bloomberg Press:2004) p.81

The Hotel Family Story:

Do you remember the hotel operator I spoke about in Chapter 5? Consider the story of Leisel Pritzker, the niece of Jay Pritzker, the key owner and patriarch of the Pritzker family who owns the $15 billion Marmon Group, which includes the Hyatt Hotels. When Jay Pritzker died in 1999 he left Leisel, who was a teenager at the time and probably not even on his radar screen, a multi-million dollar inheritance. Leisel and her legal team did not think it was enough, launching a legal battle that raged for many years, significantly impacting the operations of the company, to the point where they had to sell off assets at fire sale prices to Warren Buffett[4]. While the Family Enterprise is still in operation, it is doubtful that the family is a poster child for harmony.

I, fortunately have, experienced harmony in my family as evidenced with the death of the matriarch of my own family enterprise. My Dad, the patriarch, died tragically with a heart attack many years earlier when I was a teenager and my Mom was in her forties. I have eight brothers and sisters, and despite this adversity and some others that families go through, we successfully managed to work together harmoniously on any family or business issues that have arisen. Because we have communicated with each other for our entire life at every opportunity, good and bad, this principle has served us well. That's why I always say that: "Families and the family businesses that play together, stay together." We learned this behavior at an early age from my parents.

---

[4]   Andrew Farrell, Article reported in Forbes.com entitled "Buffett helps resolve Pritzker Family Feud", Dec. 26, 2007

CHAPTER EIGHT

HAVING FUN IN

THE DEPARTURE LOUNGE

Music held my family together through thick and thin. Upon entering the MacDonald's family store, you would very often hear the sound of musical instruments being played or singing of old Scottish songs, country music, rock and roll, blues and just about anything else. Along with our piano, our relatives, friends and customers would bring their voice, their fiddle, accordion, guitars, drums, and even their feet for step dancing. Music was played everywhere; at weddings, at square dances, and even at a funeral mass you would hear lots of singing or hear a violin or bagpipe playing a Scottish lament. My Mom attended to weddings and funerals with equal fervor because it was a grand social event. Music was the centerpiece of our family, our business and our community.

Most of all, music was fun, and every member of the family, and every generation, took part. Even if they didn't play an instrument, they could enjoy listening, or tapping their toes, or dancing along. Everyone had a great time, and it bonded us together. After a family disagreement, music helped heal the wounds, and keep the family together.

That's why music and fun is the theme of this book. The Metronome is an essential tool for practicing musicians, to ensure all the members of the band are singing from the same songbook communicating well at rehearsals in anticipation of the main performance. I refer you to **Table 1** which illustrates the comparison between the New York Philharmonic and a Family Enterprise preparing for Succession and Estate Planning.

I selected the New York Philharmonic because this orchestra performed its first concert in 1842 and has been creating beautiful music ever since, despite having many different conductors. Can you imagine what would happen if there was no plan for succession after Leonard Bernstein? The point is, the New York Philharmonic will likely continue to make great music no matter who the conductor.

Do you think that if all the members of the family were involved in crafting the future vision of the family and the business that it might be inspirational and likely to work better than if the owner developed the vision completely on her own? What about rehearsals? The vision for a family and the family enterprise when the owner (conductor) is not there cannot be done effectively in one meeting. It is unlikely that all the stakeholders would demonstrate much buy in without some input in creating this vision. This is an ongoing process which involves regular family meetings, a process of good governance and protocols for communication amongst the stakeholders.

The prospect of working on a succession and estate plan for your business and your family sounds like anything but fun. (Some individuals have confided that they would rather have a root canal!) At first glance, it looks like a lot of time and effort is focused on you dying, and leaving the stage permanently. I have to admit that early in my career I was brainwashed by sales training programs hosted by large financial institutions to scare the prospective clients into buying financial products to solve the problem. Not only did this approach make the people we met depressed, but we were also asking them to write a big cheque which depressed them even further. No wonder less than 10% of family business owners have a formal succession and estate plan and why their businesses and their families could suffer horrible unintended consequences as a result.

So why not make it fun? Why not reverse the paradigm? Let's approach this project differently, with the goal to make it fun, positive, life-affirming, and fulfilling. Let's consider that most of the benefits from this work will happen while you are alive, and some of them will happen very quickly. For example, as your family comes together to work on these issues, you will grow closer and understand each other better. There will be disagreements and even some conflict but worries and stresses will be replaced by peace of mind, and a greater sense of calm. Guided two way conversations where everyone in the family has a voice will make everyone feel heard, as well as feel good about their role when the family must continue on their own without the owner's guidance.

This process does not need to be laborious. You can take it one step at a time. The main steps are:

1. **Articulate the vision** of what you really want to have happen to your business and your family after you are gone. This might only take about an hour or two. If this was all you do, you will make better decisions going forward. Of course, it would be best if your spouse participated in this conversation because guess what? He or she secretly wanted to have this conversation many years ago. As the main beneficiary of everything you own and created during your life together, your spouse will be most affected by what happens after you are gone. We have discovered that the spouses are extremely interested in this subject for that reason, especially as the two of you get older.

Let's face it. Once you hit 60 you are in the "departure lounge". I heard this term 'departure lounge' for the first time while listening to a radio documentary broadcast from Ireland. An elderly Irish gentleman was talking about how he loved to sing and play the organ for his fellow residents in the Retirement Home on Wednesday nights. Most of the residents were preparing for the final stage of their life and he called this the departure lounge. Except that on Wednesday nights he put a smile on their faces with music.

The plane is going to leave, and it is a one-way ticket. The good news is you can have a lot of fun in the departure lounge. There can even be singing and dancing. Even better, you and your family can create your own songbook. You can write your own song and practice together, leaving a legacy, your family will be able to continue for generations.

2. **Communicate your vision**. It is not a good idea to write this particular song yourself and then leave it for the family to sing for the first time without any communication, sharing or feedback at the reading of your last will and testament. Your family will probably not like the song, and never sing it, because it affects them, they never had a voice in creating it, and they are expected to follow it. Many family businesses miss this critical step of good regular communication and as a result have failed miserably transitioning wealth and maintaining family relationships to the next generation. When I say communication, I mean two-way communication, which involves respectful listening, collaboration, and feedback on issues and concerns for each family member. Disagreement is normal and conflict is inevitable. Many successful family enterprises have regular family meetings, strong governance and conflict resolution strategies so that everyone has their voice heard.

This may sound intimidating, especially if two-way collaborative communication has not been the norm in your family, but there is an easy solution. You may be wise to hire a facilitator who is trained to work with family enterprises to act as the catalyst for this type of interaction. The facilitator acts as the metronome, keeping the family in time and in tune, so they can create great music together.

Ultimately, family members with a little bit of training and coaching can perform this role themselves.

This approach to communication is generally outside the comfort zone of the owner, who has run the business up to the present as a feudal kingdom. The autocratic style of one way communication is not likely to work when you are planning the transition of wealth generated from your family enterprise to your family members.

3. Document your plan by writing it down as a family agreement. I call this a **Family Accord**®. I suggest a binder which looks a lot like a family album (happy memories are put in family albums). This binder would contain the shared family song (Vision), a Family Chart of band members (family members) and supporting cast members (accountant, lawyer, life insurance advisor, and other key family enterprise advisors), the three circle model identifying family members, owners and management of the family business (see Exhibit 1 at the end of Chapter 4).

What is More Important? Your Family or Your Business?

This process is not for everyone, and it won't work for the un-committed. So how do you determine if you are committed? It's easy. Ask yourself this simple question: What is more important to you: your family or your business? It is a tricky question, because this is one situation where it is tough to answer both. Tragically, many owners of family businesses choose one over the other. You can't kid yourself. If you have spent all of your time at the office, and spent very little time with your family, it is difficult for you to say that your family comes first. However, if that is the case, you still have the chance to change it. If you decide that your business comes first, then fine, you don't need to do this process. What would be the point?

Let's assume that you say that your family is more important than your business. It doesn't mean that your business is not important; it just comes in a close second. That's why this kind of work is vital if you want to protect both your family and your business, because in this situation they are inextricably tied together.

There is a great book on this very issue of 'family first or business first'[1]. The key point of the book, is that you should not choose one over the other as if it were framed as a problem to be solved, but rather choose both as a third alternative through mutual inclusion and necessity. In fact, the authors call this the ultimate paradox of a family enterprise which should be managed and coped with rather than solved. The paradox is defined in the book as ". . . two sides that appear to be opposing but in fact are mutually supportive". The current thinking today in academia, supported by excellent research, is that great, enduring family enterprises which make up to 80% of the world's businesses[2] manage these paradoxes instead of trying to solve them as a problem.[3]

Engaging in two-way collaborative communication with your family, where everyone has a voice, is a way for you to prove that your family comes first. Actions speak louder than words. What you are really doing is preparing your family for the ownership and control of everything you worked your whole life to create. Remember that your spouse played a vital role regardless of whether or not he or she worked in the business.

---

[1] Amy Schuman, Stacy Stutz, and John L. Ward. *Family Business as Paradox* Palgrave MacMillan (2010): 20-23. Print.

[2] Kelin e. Gersick, John A. Davis, Marion McCollom Hampton, Ivan Lansberg, *Generation to Generation Life Cycles of the Family Business*, Harvard Business School Press, 1997, Intro. P.2

[3] Amy Schuman, Stacy Stutz, and John L. Ward. *Family Business as Paradox* Palgrave MacMillan (2010): 20-23. Print.

It is your choice. You are in the departure lounge. The plane is being fueled. Boarding may begin at any day. You can either pretend you aren't really there, or you can take a look around and realize where you are. Once you realize that you are in fact in the departure lounge, why not invite your family to join you. And then, wouldn't it be more fun, if there was singing and dancing?

How to Get Started on Your Family Agreement

1. Download the Succession Scorecard ("Do we have a problem?")

2. Download the 4 Powerful Questions ("What are the issues/opportunities?")

3. Call us to help you create your own Family Agreement at 1.877.336.3332

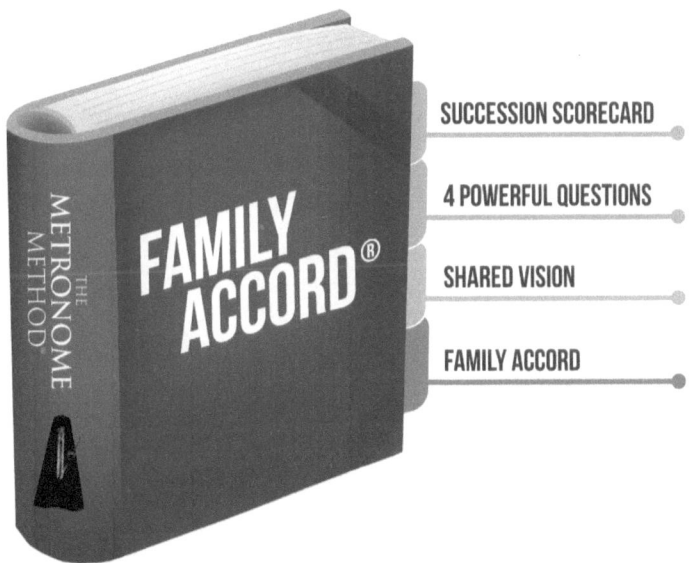

For Tools and Resources go to:
www.successionprotection.com

Exhibit 1

The Three Circle Model

Who are the stakeholders and how do they perceive their role within the Family Enterprise?

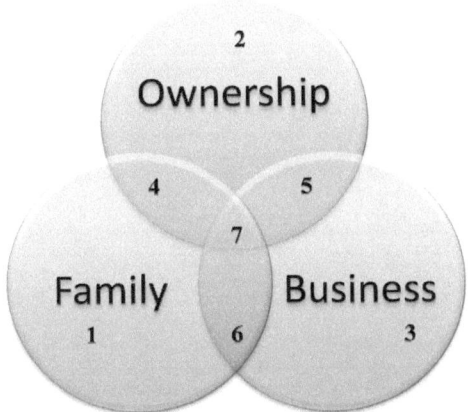

1. Family Members who are not actively involved in the business either as employees or owners.
2. External Investors who own part of the business but who do not work in it and are not members of the family.
3. Non-Family management and employees with no ownership.
4. Family Members who own shares in the business but who are not employees.
5. Owners who work in the business but who are not family members.
6. Family members who work in the business but who do not own shares.
7. Inhabiting all three circles are owners who are also family members and who work in the business.

Source: Adapted from R. Tagiuri and John A. Davis (1982) Bivalent Attributes of the Family Firm, reprinted (1996) in the Classics section of Family Business Review, Volume IX, Number 2, Summer, 199-208. Used with permission from Family Business Review, Sage Publications.

Table 1

A Model for Succession
& Estate Planning for Family Enterprises

New York Philharmonic	The Family Enterprise
Conductor (Music Director)	Owner and Founder
Sheet Music (Songbook)	Vision for Family and Enterprise
Orchestra members (Musicians)	Family members (Founder's spouse, children and their spouses)
Technical Support Staff (*Multi-Disciplinary Team)	Accountants, Lawyers, Insurance Agents, Private Wealth Advisors, Family Therapists, Facilitators
Metronome	Family Agreement (album, plan)

* *It would be beneficial to the families if the professional advisors on the Team were aware of and had training in the three circle model developed by Tagiuri and Davis referred to in Chapter 5. There is a Family Enterprise Advisor ("FEA") designation in Canada through the Institute of Family Enterprise Advisors ("IFEA") that is excellent for professional advisors to Family Enterprises.*